Explaining Effective Marketing in Contemporary Globalism

Explaining Effective Marketing in Contemporary Globalism

An Exponential Tutorial

Kelechikwu Emmanuel Oguejiofor

 www.trafford.com
North America & international
toll-free: 1 888 232 4444 (USA & Canada)
fax: 812 355 4082

ACKNOWLEDGEMENT

This book and the honor it contends should all be championed to the immense sacrifice made by those who I ought to forever be greatful to, my beloved "parents" Father "Chief Sir, Jonathan Oguejiofor (JP)" (Nwakaibeya), but most especially my beloved mother Late Lady Helen Amaka Oguejiofor (Agunwayi) , both parents hails from Oraifite, Ekwusigo Local Goverment in Anambra State, Nigeria. She was the driving force of my inner convictions. Regarless of the inefficiencies faced right here in Africa, yet I found a fearless woman right at the end of a tunnel, her life in summary, continiously inspired my pursuit for purpose in life with the fact that I must optmise her fundamental springboard that globalization did provide a powerful tool to fight all inefficiencies and with this fact, she endeared all her life striving with full tenacity in justaposition of Africa for Global excellence, such passion that I equally shared as well. Also she was an examplary role model to all her children. She believed that no matter the odds that hardworking, responsibility and deligence will somehow prevail, and on this accord. She made all sacrifice to see that her children obtained quality education . From a personal perception, I witnessed an extreme disciplinarian and a teacher turned a mere trader in our dusty contemporary african markets in order to meet the uttermost challenges every african home faced. Which were the basic provisions for basic amenities coupled with the odds that challenged responsibilities and hardworking . She grew supporting the business ventures of her husband and they later grew with high level of affluence earning both of them substantial goodwill and   the honorary titles (Agunwayi) and her husband (Nwakaibeya). Both as well respected and dedicated traders, built an empire that surely will withstand the test of time, earning them the well deserved distinctive 25years leverage on (FMCG: Fast Moving Consumer Goods), operating in Aba, Abia State,Nigeria, in Africa's most populous nation. She inspired my pursuit for purpose in life and I find hope connecting the biblical believe that all things worketh out for good to them that trust in the Lord. It is with such anchor I present this work in commeration of a "Rare Gem: A priceless gift of a lifetime" who paved way for all there is and so with the mere aim at heart. It is with such priceless inspiration that I wish to advance business stakeholders, professionals, practitioners and also including upper level graduates by utilizing a critical realistic perspective in explaning effective marketing in contemporary Globalism. And I bet you will find this work very intresting and important. In commeration of her bountiful wisdom, may her beautiful soul rest in the bossom of the lord, Adieu MaMa, Till we meet to part no more, all is well !

Contents

ABSTRACT

This paper seeks to broaden the perspective of contemporary theories on strategic marketing management. The research proposal goes on to checkmate the relevancy of theories to practice. The paper was prepared with the aim in mind to shed light on the understanding of marketing theories and its relevancy to global competitiveness. The paper put fort proper strategies on effective marketing in contemporary globalism; here contemporary theories reveal the same findings. The proposal consists and goes in dept to cover the basic yet usually ignored by marketing mangers in the areas as follows; 1) The constant changing process of business environment, 2) Strategies to strengthen company's competitive position, 3) Formulation of segmentation, Targeting, and positioning strategies, 4) Decisive decision making in areas such as finance, human aspects and many more. These 4 areas are most important and form the backbones for efficient marketing in contemporary globalism. This paper lays out each and every aspect as a research proposal to HoveHive but yet providing invaluable insights to business stakeholders. The paper provides recommendations in two folds; both theoretical and practical implications to make this research proposal more meaningful and practical enough to be adopted by HoveHive, academic world and of course not discounting those practitioners who do NOT wish to HOPE but to make things happen through effective strategic marketing management in their respective organizations.

EXECUTIVE SUMMARY

The saying goes; all good things must come to an end; however we at HoveHive refused to buy such statement. We believe that not all good things must come to an end, sometimes good things is better when persevered for a long lasting mutual beneficial relation for excellence and that is the strong DNA that each and every one of us at HoveHive possess, thus this research proposal is prepared to the Chairman of HoveHive Group who is currently spearheading a new product initiative that will cost the company nothing lesser than 500 million Naira. As the amount is a very huge sum of money, therefore it is very important to ensure readers of this proposal understand the four core concepts that are to be covered in the body of this research paper. The first section is to talk about the constant changing process of the business environment in which the company operates and decisions about how to change the marketing mix in order to succeed and reflect new strategies suitable for changing environment; second section is to discuss on ways to strengthen the competitive position of the company and discuss ways to satisfy customers and achieve performance targets according to its resources and abilities while attaining technical efficiencies as a valid leverage over contemporaries; third section of the proposal is to review the company's overall direction pertaining to the formulation of segmentation, targeting and positioning (STP) strategies of the organization and the fourth section is about how decision is made in HoveHive, which we shall conclude with decision-making about our production thru (unique selling proposition) and operations, finance, human resource management and other business issues which are more complex. Besides the above- mentioned outline, the body of this research proposal also include several figures for ease of reference. All in all, the most important piece of this research proposal is to provide a real life example and not only contribute to the body of literature theoretically but to aid easy practical hybridization for business professionals and practitioners, enabling them to easily execute the processes contained herein in such systematic way.

1.1 THE CONSTANTLY CHANGING PROCESS OF THE BUSINESS ENVIRONMENT IN WHICH THE COMPANY OPERATES AND DECISIONS ABOUT HOW TO CHANGE THE MARKETING MIX IN ORDER TO SUCCEED AND REFLECT NEW STRATEGIES SUITABLE FOR CHANGING ENVIRONMENT

Introduction

Few of our African Executive Directors visit the dusty industrial city of Lanzhou on China's Yellow River. Even fewer ventures up the narrow and dirty road that I am on today; which is also the home to one of the city's street markets. It is lined with stalls, their thin wooden poles supporting roofs and walls of dingy fabric. From beside one of them, a small boy stares at me in amazement and then runs excitedly to report this strange sight to his mother.

She sits, by a spring balance twice her age, in the cramped space that remains behind all her stocks: sacks of rice, grain, sunflower seeds and nuts and above them a rickety shelf that crowded with bags full of bright-colored which prospective customers are sniffing and tasting, before checking out the next dry-goods stall.

The boy stills stares, still goggle-eyed but I press on purposely. The next stall is piled high with melons, bananas and strange vegetables. The stallholder a young woman with long black hair is scrubbing one such vegetable over an enamel bowl full of water while at the other side a bell rings behind me, I move smartly out of the way of a bicycle pulling a steaming brazier, the size of an oil drum, from which its owner sell hot soup. I WALK on. Plastic baths of water, full of live fish jut into my path. Next, there is a stall with wooden cages full of live chicken in steel pan. In short, I am not sure what I want after a long walk and finally reached my goal: a tiny wooden kiosk with no door and a large unglazed window. Inside sits a young, attractive girl in red shirt, the street market's only seamstress. She has no sewing machine- though one day, PERHAPS, she should have saved enough to buy one but she stitches by hand with great precision.

We (Africans and Chinese) cannot speak each other's language, but I hand her the slacks that I am holding and show her how the hems have come adrift. She grasps my meaning immediately and nods exaggeratedly as if no make plan; even to someone unlucky enough not to be born Chinese, that she understands, I want to know the price, so I point to my palm with a puzzled expressions on my face. She holds up five fingers, which I guess means five Yuan. That is probably way over the going rate, but to me it is a tiny sum and I would much rather pay it than waste more time looking for another seamstress, I nod and the transaction takes place. I stand outside; there is no room for two in her small workspace so I look around as I wait. Further from the main thoroughfare, the stalls give way to people selling fruits, vegetables, oil, rice and even underwear. Further still, vendors sit on the ground, their goods spread out on a simple sheet.

For one thing, I have confirmed my belief that markets are everywhere. China is still supposed to be a communist country, but even herein Lanzhou, China I have found markets just like those in typical Africa i.e. Ariaria and Eziukwu International Market both in Aba, Abia State, Nigeria (A market ascribed as the largest trading market in West and sub Saharan Africa). Even do, the goods on sale may be far stranger herein Lanzhou, China (and the vendors perhaps less strange: there are few sights more colorful than stallholders in developing countries otherwise they are no different but huge variety of goods and sellers, from which a throng of customers somehow make choices.

In actuality, choice defines markets, even in an authoritarian country like China. The girl in the red shirt was not forced to mend my hem; nor was I forced to accept the price. Either of us could have vetoed the bargain- she decided to wait for another customer and I may have looked for a repair somewhere else. You cannot isn't MARKET or else both sides simply walks away. Collective bargaining is paramount as consumers constantly demand cheaper price irrespective of exceeding quality assurance and sellers turns to be tactical in other to cover cost and make "profit" Which is somewhat fundamentals of any business enterprise.

The above scenario is not a fairytale story, it is actually happening to us in our daily life without us realizing. The scenario also describes how strategic marketing takes place by ordinary people in a *simple* market place. Even in the simple market place, traders know what strategic marketing is all about and blend in the overall marketing mix like most of the established organization does. The only difference between the smaller traders in comparison with the established organization is that small traders practice marketing mix in a very loose way however an established organization such as HoveHive has to unveil strategic plans to enable them to track their marketing mix in a more proper, structured and systematic way and even enable track the actual return on investment (ROI) by tracking the actual marketing campaigns.

The Marketing Mix

The marketing mix is the term given to a set of variables that a marketer can exercise control over in creating an offering for exchange (Blackie, 2008; Carson 2009 & Hallet, 2009). Various frameworks for the marketing mix have evolved over time, including:

- The 4 Ps framework – product, price, promotion and place (place is more easily understood as distribution). The 4 Ps framework was the first approach to the marketing mix.
- The 5 Ps framework which evolved from the 4 Ps model by adding a fifth P, 'people', to the 4 Ps framework.
- The 6 Ps framework which added 'process' to the 5 Ps framework.
- The 7 Ps framework which added 'physical evidence' to the 6 Ps framework.

Marketers cannot act with complete freedom in determining their marketing mix. They are governed by the costs of implementing the various marketing mix options, as well as the forces at play in the marketing environment. They are also governed by the people in their organization. There is little point creating something that is simply not possible to implement (Bradsher, 2007 & Cinnota, 2009).

This research proposal had discussed on ways how business process take place and even small stallholders blend around with their own marketing mix by making their business relevant to the ever changing market as stipulated in the scenario above in China how our African

Executive Director can get his product/service done even though both do not speak in each other's language but business transaction become possible through elements of these various marketing mix / frameworks. It is important to remember that– whatever marketing mix framework an organization applies or considers – is ultimately about a total focus on servicing the needs and wants of the customer.

In the following sections to come, this research paper will cover ways to strengthen the competitive position of the company and discuss ways to satisfy customer and achieve performance targets according to its resources and abilities.

1.2 WAYS TO STRENGTHEN THE COMPETITIVE POSITION OF THE COMPANY AND DISCUSS WAYS TO SATISFY CUSTOMERS AND ACHIEVE PERFORMANCE TARGETS ACCORDING TO ITS RESOURCES AND ABILITIES

Who/which organizations in this world have infinite resources? Even the most powerful nation(s), most sophisticated organization(s) and even the richest people have no unlimited resources. For example; the richest person in the world wants more than 24 hours in a day but that is not possible as all of us is fully aware that no matter how rich an individual or an organization is, We only have 24 hours, as simple as that- period. The same things apply to organization, most organizations want to produce millions of products each year but reality is, they are faced with limited resources. Thus, let us take a look how the conventional 4ps' has evolved into 7ps' as follows (Finn, 2007 & & Hallet, 2009):

- Product
- Price
- Promotion
- People
- Process
- Physical Evidence
- Partners *(HoveHive is required to utilize this particular marketing mix in line with unique selling proposition USP to achieve their*

strategic vision as *"**Top Choice National and International Franchise Alliance by 2020**")*

The Marketing Environment

The marketing environment refers to all of the internal and external forces that affect a marketer's ability to create, communicate, deliver and exchange offerings of value (Ironside, 2007). The factors and forces within the marketing environment can be classified as belonging to the internal environment, the micro environment, and the macro environment. The internal environment refers to the organization itself and the factors that are directly controllable by the organization (Chester, 2009). The micro environment comprises the forces and factors at play inside the industry in which the marketer operates. Micro-environmental factors affect all parties in the industry, including suppliers, distributors, customers and competitors. The macro environment comprises the larger-scale societal forces that influence not only the industry in which the marketer operates, but all industries. Macro-environmental factors include political forces, economic forces, sociocultural forces, technological forces and legal forces. This macro-environmental framework has been called the PESTL (for political, economic, sociocultural, technological, legal) framework. Micro-environmental and macro-environmental forces are outside of the organization and, while they can be influenced, they cannot be directly controlled (Featherstone, 2009; Hallet, 2009 & Walters & Lindhe, 2009).

Effective marketers must seek to monitor, understand, respond to, and influence their environment. This is a complex task and encompasses all of marketing.

Environmental analysis is an analytical approach that involves breaking the marketing environment into smaller parts for better understanding that aids decisive decision making. This part introduces key considerations for an environmental analysis in order to provide you with insights into some of the things that effective marketers need to understand (Sibilin, 2009).

Herein we have discussed the internal and external environments and conclude with an explanation of how to conduct a situation analysis of the organization's overall marketing environment. The situation analysis and the organization's objectives form the basis of effective marketing planning.

Internal Environment

The internal environment refers to the parts of the organization, the people and the processes used to create, communicate, deliver and exchange offerings that have value. The internal environment is directly controllable by the organization. A thorough understanding of the internal environment ensures that marketers understand the organization's strengths and weaknesses. Strengths and weaknesses are internal factors that positively and negatively affect the organization's ability to compete in the marketplace. Typically marketers seek to minimize weaknesses and maximize strengths (Narver & Slater, 2010).

The most successful organizations are those with a market orientation. This means that all parts of the organization are focused on creating and delivering value for their market. While this may seem simple, it is often very difficult in practice. Organizations consist of people, groups, departments and complex interrelationships. At times these can work against each other, rather than with each other. In reality, the internal environment of any organization is affected by the personal and political natures of the people who make it up. It is important to be aware that as organizational complexity increases, so does the potential for conflict. Marketers need to understand the parts of the organization and the processes that are in place. The main parts of a typical organization include (Passmore, 2008; Shoebriedge, 2007a & Shoebriedge, 2007b):

- Senior management – responsible for making decisions about the overall objectives and strategy of the organization
- Middle management – typically responsible for a department or a geographic region. Middle management makes decisions about the overall objectives and strategy of the department or geographic region for which they have responsibility. Their aim is to make sure the objectives for their department or region are aligned with the objectives of the organization as a whole.
- Functional departments – organizations can be structured around functional departments and/ or regions. If you are a business student you will study many of these functions during your degree. Functional departments may include:
    - marketing
    - sales
    - research and development
    - customer service

- distribution/logistics
- manufacturing
- finance
- human resources
- administration.

To be successful, all of the parts of the internal environment should work together towards one common goal. This is most likely to occur when each person and department understands their contribution and the contribution of other departments. The marketing department is best positioned to understand what customers' value. It is the marketing department's role to collaborate with the human resources department to ensure that all members within an organization understand their role in creating, communicating, delivering and exchanging offerings that have value, marketing, like all other parts, processes and people in an organization, must work to achieve the overall organizational objectives and must always demonstrate how it does so (Napolitano, 2007 & Shoebriedge, 2007b).

Micro Environment

The micro environment consists of customers, clients, partners and competitors. Unlike, the internal environment, the micro environment is not directly controllable by the organization. The organization can, however, exert some influence on the customers, clients, partners, competitors and other parties that make up its industry and it can influence satisfaction by improving its complaint handling procedures (Ironside, 2007).

In one way or another, all of the factors in the micro environment affect the marketer. In analyzing the micro environment, marketers need to consider customers and clients; partners, including suppliers; and competitors (Levitt, 1983 & Medcalf, 2009).

- Customers and Clients
- Suppliers
- Competitors

The Macro Environment

The organization itself and all of the forces within the micro environment operate within a larger environment known as the macro environment. The macro environment encompasses the factors outside of the industry that influence the survival of the organization. In practice, the macro environment can be at any geographic level including local, state, country or regional (e.g. The West of Africa (Ecowas), the Asia-Pacific or the European Union (Levitt, 1983 & Medcalf, 2009).

In some cases it is possible for marketers to influence macro-environmental factors. However, these factors will always remain beyond a marketer's control. For example, a company can lobby government to reduce the tax on wine but they cannot directly control the rate set by the government. Failure to plan based on emerging trends can lead to business closure. Effective marketers continually monitor the environment, adapting and changing offers where necessary in response to changes in the macro environment (Murdoch, 2008). News services, business and investment media, libraries, the internet and industry associations are all avenues to inform marketers of developments in the macro environment. Key environmental factors that marketers need to consider when analyzing the marketing environment include political, economic, sociocultural, technological and legal forces. (This view of the macro environment is commonly abbreviated to 'PESTL'.)(Bradsher, 2007; Carson, 2009 & Feathersrone, 2009). The key considerations are summarized in figure1.1.

Political

The political arena has a huge influence upon businesses and the spending power of consumers. Marketers must consider:
1. The stability of the political environment
2. The influence of government policy, laws and regulation
3. Government trade agreements such as ECOWAS
4. Taxation and government rebate policies (i.e. Distribution Finance Scheme) DFS

Economic

Marketers need to understand the economy in the short and long terms. Marketers must consider:
1. Interest rates, economic growth (gross domestic product) and consumer confidence
2. Income levels, savings, credit and spending levels
3. The level of inflation, employment and unemployment
4. Exchange rates and balance of trade.

Sociocultural

Social and cultural influences have a large influence on businesses. Marketers must understand:
1. Religion, culture, subcultures, values, attitudes and beliefs
2. Population trends including age, household size and composition, marriage and divorce trends, places lived, ethnicity and health.

Technological

Technology is vital for competitive advantage. Marketers must consider:
1. Whether offerings can be made more cheaply and to a better standard of quality using new technologies
2. Whether technology can be used to innovate
3. Whether distribution or communication can be improved using technology.

Legal

Marketers need to understand legal and regulatory influences such as:
1. Laws including the Competition and Consumer Act, The Privacy Act, The Spam Act, The Sale of Goods Act and the Prices Surveillance Act
2. Regulations from industry bodies such as the National Food and Drugs Agency (NAFDAC), Standard Organization of Nigeria (SON)

Figure 1.1: The macro environment

In short, if HoveHive wants to succeed in the Nigerian environment that they are in, it is extremely important for them to thoroughly examine on the 7Ps' of present marketing, internal environment and external environment carefully. It is because by strengthen the company with limited resource is not the only obstacle faced by HoveHive but all organizations around. Thus, the best (survivor of the fittest of any organization) is the one that is able to position itself well with their limited resources would be the first step to achieve their organizational marketing goal.

1.3 FORMULATION OF SEGMENTATION, TARGETING AND POSITIONING (STP) STRATEGIES OF THE COMPANY

Knowing the Market

In the early section of this research proposal, the author had defined a market as a group of customers with heterogeneous needs and wants. This is a very broad definition, while the write up narrows down by allowing us to see the overall market could be broken down into consumer markets and business markets. Business markets could then, for example, be further broken down into reseller markets, producer markets, government markets and institutional markets (Finn, 2007).

These distinctions between markets are useful. As we shall come to understand as we work through this research proposal, there are many marketing issues specific to organizations that market to consumers and those that market to particular types of organizations. Many organizations target both consumers and businesses, and usually apply different strategies to each sector. However, the concepts of the consumer market and the business market are so general that they can only be used in the broadest sense to help an organization formulate a marketing strategy to target potential customers (Cinotta, 2009; Featherstone, 2009 & Walters & Lindhe, 2009). Consumers and businesses vary considerably in their needs, wants and demands, and it is virtually impossible for an organization to successfully appeal to every consumer or business, these understanding created by this detailed analysis is crucial to creating, communicating and delivering product offerings of value (see figure 1.2).

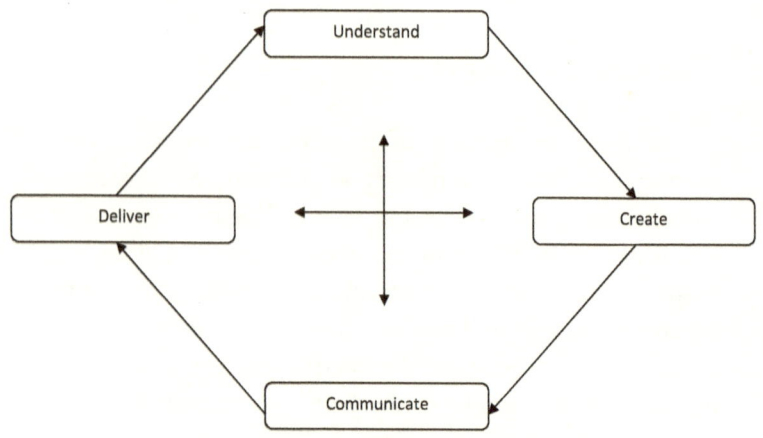

Figure 1.2: Understanding target market
segments is crucial to creating,
Communicating and delivering product offerings of value

Target Marketing

There are various ways to view the market and the particular perspective an organization takes has a pervasive influence on all of its marketing activities. However, the following key points are the main components when it comes to target marketing; the 3 points are listed as follows (Sibilin, 2009 & Shoebriedge, 2007a):

1. Buyers have common wants, needs and demands.
2. Buyers have unique wants, needs and demands.

3. The market contains subgroups – known as market segments – defined by similarities in regards to certain characteristics.

The Target Marketing Process

The target marketing process is a fundamental component of marketing strategy for any organization. The process involves three main stages, with each requiring detailed analysis and decision making (Shoebriedge, 2007a & Shoebriedge, 2007b). This summary process is illustrated in figure 1.3.

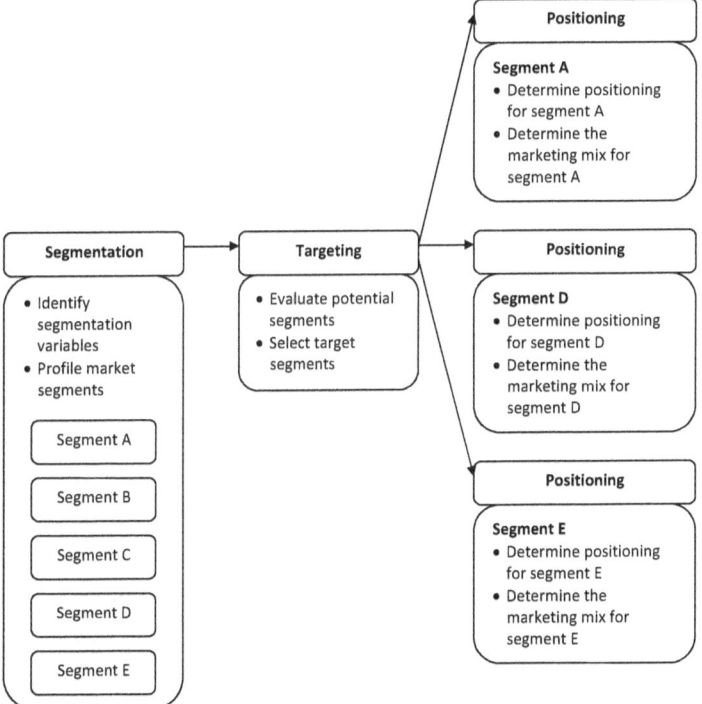

Figure 1.3: The Target marketing process

Market Segmentation

The first stage of the target marketing process is market segmentation. As shown in figure 1.4, there are two steps in the market segmentation phase: identifying variables that can be used to define meaningful market segments; and profiling the market segments so they can be accessed in the second stage of the target marketing process (Murdoch, 2008; Passmore, 2008 & Walters & Lindhe, 2009).

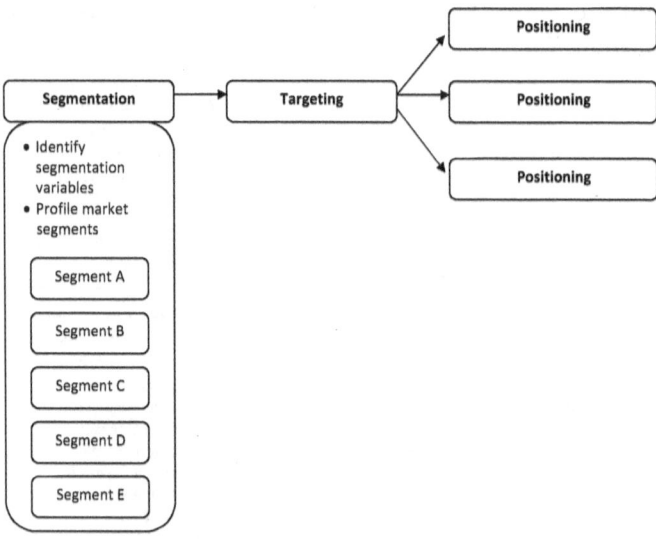

Figure 1.4: The Target marketing process
stage 1: Market segmentation

Following are the variables marketers take into account before segmenting; following are the different segments that marketers break it down so that it is easier for them to focus on which segment to concentrate on (Bradsher, 2007; Chester, 2009 & Levitt, 1983):

Identify Segmentation Variables
- Segmenting consumer markets
- Geographic Segmentation
- Demographic Segmentation
- Psychographic Segmentation
- Behavioral Segmentation

Market Targeting

Having identified and described the range of possible market segments to which an organization might direct its offer, the second stage in the process is that of market targeting. This stage involves a systematic examination of the range of possible market segments, their potential sales volume and revenues, and the relative ability of the organization to satisfy the expectations of members of these market segments. This step also requires a close understanding of competitors, and how their offerings are seen by potential target market segments. In this context, it is important to realize that no company or brand can be all things to all people, especially when considering the vast array of potential customers and their diverse needs, wants and demands (Chester, 2009; Cinotta, 2009 & Medcalf, 2009).

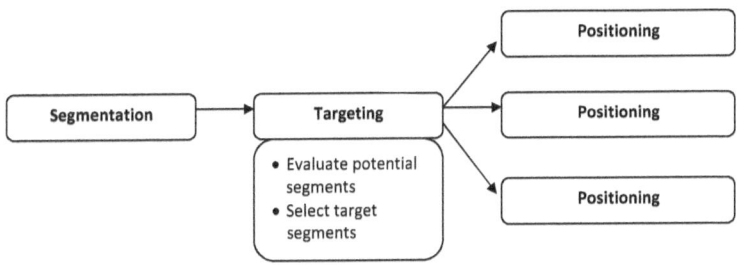

Figure 1.5: The target marketing process
stage 2: Market targeting

Each of the strategies of undifferentiated marketing, differentiated marketing and specialized marketing offers advantages and disadvantages, which make the choice of target marketing strategy crucial for long-term survival and profitability. The choice of appropriate targeting strategy ultimately depends on the following (Murdoch, 2008, Passmore, 2008, Sibilin, 2009 & Shoebriedge, 2007a):

- An understanding of the size and attractiveness of the market segments that have been identified
- The organization's ability to service and compete for the chosen market segments
- Evaluate potential segments
- Sales Potential
- Competitive Situation
- Cost Structure
- Select Target Markets

Products: Goods, Services and Ideas

From the beginning of this research proposal, the marketing process was shown to comprise creating, communicating, delivering and exchanging offerings that have value for customers. A product is defined as a good, service or idea offered to the market for exchange. Without a product, a marketer has nothing to offer. On the other side of the exchange, potential customers require products to satisfy functional, social and psychological needs, wants and demands. The core concept is that both parties must gain value from the exchange (Napolitano, 2007 & Narver & Slater, 2010).

Goods are physical, tangible offerings that are capable of being delivered to a customer. Because it is tangible, you can see, touch, taste and smell a good (depending on what it is). The purchase of a good usually involves the transfer of ownership from marketer to customer (Narver & Slater, 2010).

The Total Product Concept

Products have many different features that can provide value for customers, clients, partners and society at large. At the most basic level, marketers must ensure that the product attributes satisfy the needs and wants of potential buyers. It is this ability to satisfy a need or want that makes the product of value to potential customers. To make a product of more value than competing offerings, the marketer must take a more comprehensive view of the product. To understand how the product's value is perceived by potential customers, it is useful to describe the product in terms of product (Levitt, 1983; Murdoch, 2008 & Sibilin, 2009). This view of the product is known as the total product concept and is illustrated in figure 1, 5.

The total product concept is a way of viewing a product as the totality of value and benefits it provides to the customer. Products are offered to the market to be an answer to the customer's problem of an unsatisfied need or want.

Figure 1.5: The target product concept

From figure 1.5, we can see the 4 key components that make up target product concept and they are listed as follows as suggested by (Levitt, 1983; Murdoch, 2008 & Sibilin, 2009):

The Core Product
- The Expected Product
- The Augmented Product
- The Potential Product

1.4 DECISION-MAKING ABOUT PRODUCTION AND OPERATIONS, FINANCE, HUMAN RESOURCE MANAGEMENT AND OTHER BUSINESS ISSUES IN A COMPLEX SITUATION

From beginning until this section, this research proposal has emphasized that marketing is not a linear process that begins with an idea, proceeds to a plan and ends with successful implementation of the plan. This purely means, marketing department is not static by itself and marketing as business unit (BU) by itself needs to have proper communication channels with other business units such as productions, operations, finance, human resource and other business issues especially in today's hyper-competitive market. Rather, marketing is an ongoing and interrelated process of understanding, creating, communicating and delivering offerings. Thus, it is impossible for any organization to succeed, if their marketing does not communicate with human resource and production so on and so forth. If that happens, this disease will slowly spread out and ultimately the organization will collapse. As this research proposal is very much related to strategic marketing, author will focus more on understanding, planning, implementation and evaluation although decision making about production and operations, human resource management and other business are equally important.

As witness, in the opening sentence of the section it is vital for marketing as a business unit to communicate with other business units, however as a marketing manager-You first need is to ensure your department co-ordinate well. The main activities of marketing department in any organization must undertake in relation to marketing are (Passmore, 2008 & Sibilin, 2009):

- Develop a detailed understandings of the market
- Plan how to achieve the organization's goals
- Implement the plan
- Continuously evaluate marketing performance.

In reality, marketers continually refine and adapt each and every aspects of their offerings based on the changing marketing environment and evaluation of their marketing program to date. The management task of understanding the market, and planning, implementing and evaluating marketing activities is known as STRATEGIC MARKETING MANAGEMENT. Strategic marketing management aims to ensure that the organization achieves its marketing objectives by maximizing the value obtained from the marketing exchange for the organization itself and its customers, clients, partners (both internal and external) and society at large. Based on a sound marketing of the fundamental concepts related to the market and marketing, the organization can formulate a marketing plan to achieve the organization's marketing activities. Putting the plan into action is the implementation part of marketing (Narver & Slater, 2010; Sibilin, 2009 & Shoebriedge, 2007b). Just as implementation requires a marketing plan, a plan cannot ignore the realities of implementation. There is little point in having a plan that is impossible to implement or goals that are impossible achieve. In this section, author will discuss steps the organization can take to maximize the likelihood that the marketing plan can be implemented effectively. This research proposal also notes the risks that can affect the success of the marketing plan in achieving the organization's objectives.

Marketers do not leave in the world of denial, in actuality of all profession marketers are labeled as chameleon which they can easily adapt to the environment. There are no marketers that succeed or do very well in their industry if they cannot manage both internal and external environment. Let's take step backward before this research proposal move on to marketing planning. As the headline of this section suggest, marketers have to liaise not only with external stakeholders however internal stakeholders are equally important if not more. A very classic example will be, let's say the marketing team is going to launch a new product the marketing director has to liaise with productions and operation, finance, human resource department, and probably logistic as well. The marketing director needs to communicate with production and operations so that the products produced are in line to customers' demands. On top of that, just imagine without communication to production and operation demand the department may over or under produce the end goods for the launch and it is going to be disaster. Now, the next question is why is it important to communicate with finance and human resource department? Communications with these two departments are equally important as finance will let the marketing director know how much is allocated budget for the launch so that no money is over invested; whilst the communication with human resource is to ensure that during the launch date, there are enough staffs to support the overall launch and human resource director will also ensure the right people is placed at the right job in order to avoid redundancy as that is an overhead to the organization.

Apart of the proper channel communications, in order to achieve the marketing goal of the organization, clear marketing objectives are the roadmap to success. The concept of marketing objectives will be familiar from this research proposal. Most for-profit marketing organizations share the goals of profits, market share growth and customer retention (Blackie, 2008; Hallet, 2009 & Napolitano, 2007). This research proposal will dedicate some discussions to these objectives now and then look at a proven model for creating effective objectives and those key points are listed as follows:

- Profit
- Market share growth
- Customer Retention
- Societal Objectives
- Marketing Implementation

It is tempting to assume that once the marketing plan is formulated, implementation will proceed in a straightforward manner. There are, however, numerous complexities that make implementing marketing problematic. Additionally, new information is likely to come to light that requires constant refinements of the marketing plan (Chester, 2009).

In the second part of this section, we will consider some of the things that marketers can do to maximize the likelihood that the marketing plan will be successfully implemented or not, the key factors that need to take into consideration as posited by (Finn, 2007; Ironside, 2007; Levitt, 1983 & Passmore, 2008):

- Potential Internal Barriers
- Inertia
- Poor Coordination and Cooperation
- A short-term Outlook
- Environmental Factors
- Maximizing Success

Planning

There is an old adage that 'those who fail to plan, plan to fail'. This recognizes the importance of planning ahead of implementation. Research shows that organizations that plan perform better than organizations that do no plan.

Plans that effectively communicate strategies and objectives are documents that outline what needs to be done, by whom and when, to achieve agreed upon objectives. Marketing plans typically contain action plans to be implemented by departmental and line managers. Ideally, marketing plans will include schedules and specific actions to be taken so that managers who are responsible for implementation (but not involved directly with strategic planning) have a clear plan forward, and a clear idea of what is expected, and of whom (Narver & Slater, 2010; Sibilin, 2009 & Shoebriedge, 2007a).

Plans can help marketers focus on the longer term. Rather than focusing on the next week or month, planning requires marketers to think about this year and the next few years. The planning process requires marketers to monitor their competitions. When trying to think about the competition, marketers use their market intelligence to think about the possible ways that competitors may act. Marketers often develop contingencies to identify the different ways that competitors may act. Contingency planning requires managers and other to think ahead of things that might not go as planned and to have strategies in place to deal with them. Proper contingency planning helps organizations both identify possible problems (and opportunities) and respond quickly and appropriately to them (Murdoch, 2008 & Sibilin, 2009).

Plans help marketers to develop priorities and focus efforts on achieving specific goals and objectives. The planning process requires marketers to think about their customers and this often means that marketers focus on targeting their primary customer. The planning process helps marketers to understand which marketing approaches work and which do not work for their organizations (Murdoch, 2008 & Walters & Lindhe, 2009).

1.5 CONCLUSIONS

By writing this research paper had benefited HoveHive Group and most importantly provided a workable and practical framework. The journey of completing this research paper has been outstanding as all the goals that need to be met have been fully achieved. This research paper has accomplished what it should be achieving which it has laid out the foundation for a successful strategic marketing management by solving the issues within 1) the constantly changing process of the business environment in which the company operates and decisions about how to change the marketing mix in order to succeed and reflect new strategies suitable for the changing environment; 2) Discuss on ways to strengthen the competitive position of the company and discuss ways to satisfy customers and achieve performance targets according to its resources and abilities; 3) Explained insights of the proposal that reviewed the overall company's direction pertaining to the formulation of segmentation, targeting and positioning (STP) strategies of the organization and 4) fourth section is about how decision is made at HoveHive which we had covered the decision-making about production and operations, finance, human resource management and other business issues in a complex situation All the 4 sections have been widely discussed and it can be an asset to HoveHive enabling them achieve their strategic vision as "Top Choice National and International Franchise Alliance by 2020",also help understanding and learning within the academic world and of course not discounting those practitioners who do NOT wish to, HOPE but to make things happen through effective strategic marketing management in their respective organization.

REFERENCES

Bradsher, K. 2007. "Toyota ends GM's reign as leader in global sales." International Herald Tibune, 24 April, www.iht.com.

Blackie, T. 2008. "Global ambitions." BRW, 31 January, p.50.

Carson, V. 2009. "Packer's US ambition thwarted again." Business Today, 13 March, www.businesstoday.com.

Chester, R. 2009. "Recession winners at low end market." Courier Mail, 4-5 April, p.4.

Cinotta, K. 2009. "Smart brands in tough time." Professional Marketing, Jan-Mar, p.30; St. George Bank corporate website, www.stgeorge.com.au.

Finn, H. 2007. "The Short Blacks" Colmar Brunton Submission for the AMSRS Research Effectiveness Awards.

Featherstone, T. 2009. "Slow to stationery." BRW, 26 March- 29 April, p.87.

Hallet, A 2009. "We have lift off." New Zealand Management, April, p.19.

Ironside, R. 2007. "Qantas queues "the worst"." Courier Mail, 16 November, www.abc.net.au.

Levitt, T. 1983. "The Marketing Imagination." The Free Press: New York.

Medcalf, G. 2009. "Tightening the screws" NZMarketing, December-January, pp.26-31.

Murdoch, G. 2008. "End of a dog dynasty." Globe and Mail, 22 October, p.A2.

Napolitano, M. 2007. "Warehouse management: how to be a lean, mean cross-docking machine." Logistics Management, www.logisticsmgt.com.

Narver, J. C and Slater, S. F. 2010. "The effect of a market orientation on business profitability." Journal of Marketing, 54 (4), pp. 20-35.

Passmore, D. 2008. "Pizza, DVD, book sales rise despite tough time." NZMarketing.

Sibilin, A. 2009. "Don't believe it." BRW, 19-25 March, p.45.

Shoebriedge, N. 2007a. "Marketing goes facial." BRW, 22 Nov- 12 December, p.29.

Shoebriedge, N. 2007b. "Marketing's moment of truth." BRW, 26 March- 29 April, p.76.

Walters, K and Lindhe, J. 2009. "The new consumer." BRW, 19-25 February, pp.18-23.

AUTHORS BIOGRAPHICAL NOTES

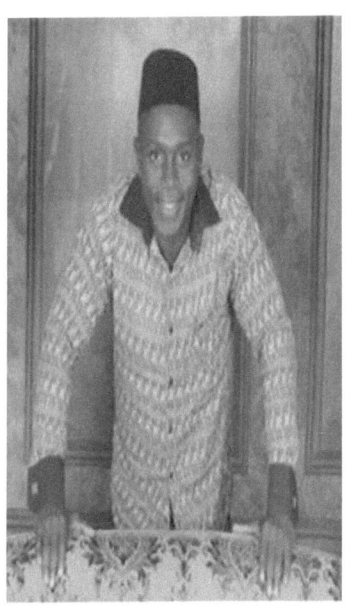

Mr. Kelechikwu Emmanuel, Oguejiofor is a Nigerian, International Business Consultant. A pioneer for sustainable business competitiveness and commitment to position Africa for Global Excellence. Emmanuel is an author of international selling book "Mastering the art of sustainable business competitiveness". He graduated with Distinction (First Class Honors) BA Hons in International Business from Nottingham Business School and with scholarship merits earned an MBA from University of Derby. He has then developed exponential competency and expertise that severed him well with various professional accolades, including Membership Grade of Chartered Management Institute and Membership of Academy of International Business. Currently, he leads top level technocrats as Chief Executive Director at HoveHive, an imprint of products and services from emerging chartered management brand operating as an auspices of Joenatex Interbiz Limited (A family trading company in Aba, Abia State, Nigeria holding distinctive 25years leverage in fast moving consumer goods). Under his lead, HoveHive aspires to achieve their 5 years strategic vision as **"Top Choice National and International Franchise Alliance" by 2020**